Laura Wasilowski

Fuse-and-Tell
JOURNAL QUILTS

Create Your Story in Cloth

C&T PUBLISHING

Text copyright © 2008 by Laura Wasilowski

Artwork copyright © 2008 by C&T Publishing, Inc.

Publisher: AMY MARSON

Creative Director: GAILEN RUNGE

Acquisitions Editor: JAN GRIGSBY

Editor: LYNN KOOLISH

Technical Editors: AMANDA SIEGFRIED and CAROLYN AUNE

Copyeditor/Proofreader: WORDFIRM INC.

Cover Designer: KRISTEN YENCHE

Book Designer: ROSE SHEIFER-WRIGHT

Production Coordinators: KIRSTIE L. PETTERSEN and KIERA LOFGREEN

Illustrator: TIM MANIBUSAN

Photography by LUKE MULKS and DIANE PEDERSEN of C&T Publishing unless otherwise noted

Published by C&T Publishing, Inc., P.O. Box 1456, Lafayette, CA 94549

Library of Congress Cataloging-in-Publication Data

Wasilowski, Laura,

   Fuse-and-tell journal quilts : create your story in cloth / Laura Wasilowski.

      p. cm.

   Summary: "Much like a journal or photo album, quilts illustrate the stories of our lives. In Fuse-and-Tell Quilts projects depict personal stories in the form of small art quilts. These journal quilts are template for readers to follow when turning their own stories into quilts"--Provided by publisher.

   Includes bibliographical references.

   ISBN 978-1-57120-502-5 (paper trade : alk. paper)

   1. Patchwork--Patterns. 2. Quilting--Patterns. 3. Diaries--Authorship. I. Title.

   TT835.W3737 2008

   746.46'041--dc22

                              2007042621

Printed in China

10 9 8 7 6 5 4 3 2 1

DEDICATION

*To those who inspire my artwork:
my family and friends*

ACKNOWLEDGMENTS

I wish to thank C&T Publishing for producing the product that made this book possible, fast2fuse. Thank you to my editor, Lynn Koolish, and the entire C&T staff. You make book publishing fun! My appre-ciation goes to my fellow Chicago School of Fusing faculty members, talented experts in the fine art of fusing. I am also grateful to my students, who always teach me more than I do them. And a special thanks to my husband, Steve, and children, Gus and Louise, who are a constant source of entertainment.

Contents

Introduction

The journal quilt is like no other art form in contemporary life.

THE FUSIBLE JOURNAL QUILT

Quilts are diaries in cloth. Whether geometric or pictorial, they tell of happy memories, sad events, funny anecdotes, or flights of fancy. Every fabric choice and every design decision illustrates the quiltmaker's story, like a journal in cloth.

For me, this combination of journal and quilt is exhilarating! I am enticed by the familiar feel of cloth and the lure of an entrancing story. I want to touch the fabric and tell the tale. The journal quilt is like no other art form in contemporary life. It has both the warmth of fabric and the emotion of a personal story.

EVERY TALE DESERVES A QUILT

This book presents six fusible journal quilts from my own riveting life. You are welcome to use my journal entries and make them your own. Or you can adapt the construction techniques presented and tell your own outlandish tales.

The method for creating each of these journal quilts is fusing. Fusing is a fast, easy way to assemble a wall quilt without sewing seams, using templates, or following a pattern. Information in the next chapter prepares you for the making of these projects, and Completing the Creation (page 54) explains easy methods of finishing the fused journal quilts.

Additional examples of journal quilts and inspirational sources are pictured throughout the book.

What better way to document your life stories than with a journal quilt? And what easier way to make that quilt than with fun, fast fusing? Every tale deserves a quilt, and every quilt has a story behind it.

BLUE CHAIR IN THE LIBRARY WITH A CANDLESTICK, 34″ × 39″, Laura Wasilowski

Fascinating Fusing Facts:
MATERIALS AND TOOLS FOR THE FUSIBLE JOURNAL QUILT

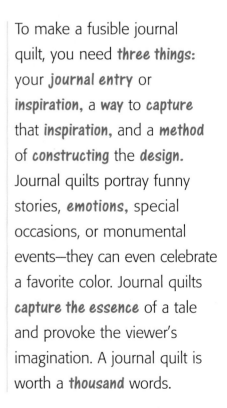

Sketch for *Leaves #1:*
Capture your inspiration in a sketch.

To make a fusible journal quilt, you need **three things:** your **journal entry** or **inspiration,** a **way** to **capture** that **inspiration,** and a **method** of **constructing** the **design.** Journal quilts portray funny stories, **emotions,** special occasions, or monumental events—they can even celebrate a favorite color. Journal quilts **capture the essence** of a tale and provoke the viewer's imagination. A journal quilt is worth a **thousand** words.

LEAVES #1, 28″ × 52″, Laura Wasilowski

YOUR JOURNAL

Every artist has a method of collecting and recording the ideas that inspire their quilts. This collection point of creative and visual descriptions may be a journal, a diary, or a sketchbook. Some artists rely on photos, paper patterns, or written descriptions of the design. There are also artists who collect fabric swatches and work directly with the fabric itself. Then there are the dreamers, like me, who rely on visualization and collect ideas in their mind. (Be forewarned: This method accounts for many traffic accidents.)

Choose fabrics with color that penetrates material so no white edges show.

TRANSLATING CREATIVE DESCRIPTIONS

No matter which system of recording you choose, your memories and impressions of everyday life are quilt material. All you need is a means of translating your ideas into fabric. Each project in this book offers a different method of transforming your inspirations into cloth. There is free-cutting, collage building, improvisational placement, shape shifting a pattern, and enlarging a sketch.

Try each method to find the process that works best for you and that works best for the quilt design. Adapt these easy techniques to your own quilt ideas, and soon you'll have beautiful pieces of fused artwork.

FUSING MATERIALS AND TECHNIQUES

Fabric Choices

The design elements in fused journal quilts are not finished with stitching. In this raw-edge, or fused-appliqué, technique, the edges of the cut elements are visible. For this reason, a tightly

woven fabric that does not fray gives a better finish. A fabric where the color penetrates completely provides consistent color around the edges of the fused elements. These characteristics are found in hand-dyed and batik fabrics. Avoid printed fabrics with a wrong side that is almost white. This white edge will appear around each element and detract from the design. Many of the quilts in this book were made with hand-dyed fabrics from my company, Artfabrik, Inc. (see Resources, page 63).

Do not use permanent-press fabrics; they will not bond well with the fusible glue. Wash fabrics before fusing to remove any finishing treatments. Iron

the fabric flat, and pull off any stray threads that may get trapped by fusible web. Save all the scraps, or confetti, from your projects for random acts of fusing (page 49) or collages made with the fusible leftovers. A fused fabric can be used today or years from now. It never loses its fusibility!

Fusibles

Fusible glue is a real boon to the creator of journal quilts and art of quilts in general. Activated by the heat of an iron, the glue will adhere, or fuse, to fabric. A fused fabric can be cut into any shape imaginable and can then be fused to another piece of fabric. There

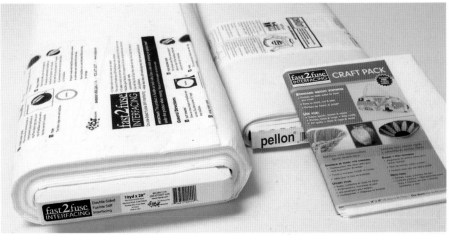
Fusible web and fast2fuse

are two fusible products that make the journal quilts in this book possible: fusible web and fast2fuse.

● USING FUSIBLE WEB

Fusible web glue usually comes on white paper called *release paper* (see Pressing Aids, page 9). Fusible web measures about 17" wide and is found in quilt shops or in the interfacing department of your fabric store. I recommend Wonder-Under (regular weight) or TransWeb. Read the directions that come with the web, or follow the directions below. Store unused fusible web in a cool, dry place.

Wash and iron your fabric before using it for fusible quilts. Cut the fusible web slightly smaller than the fabric. Place the glue side (the rough side) of the paper on the **wrong** side of the fabric. Iron in a slow glide for 7–10 seconds with a hot (cotton setting), dry iron. Let the paper and fabric cool for 15–45 minutes. (Humidity affects the removal of the paper, and the glue may need time to recrystallize.)

Fuse web to fabric with hot, dry iron.

Test to see whether the glue has transferred to the fabric by peeling up the paper at one corner. If the glue has not transferred or appears gummy, reapply the iron for an additional 7 seconds. Let the fabric cool. To remove the paper, slip your hand between the fabric and paper, and smoothly swipe off the paper, keeping it in one sheet. **Save this release paper—it plays an**

important role in the construction of fused journal quilts.

After it cools, remove release paper in one sheet.

Do not over-fuse the fabric. Too much heat for too long will damage the glue and burn it into the fabric. When composing a quilt, *fuse-tack* elements in place for about 5 seconds, and then remove the iron. Once you've completed the composition, *steam set* the glue for 10 seconds to fix it in place.

Note: If you are having difficulty removing the release paper after ironing, there may be a problem with the silicon lubricant applied to the paper. For your next piece of fabric, separate the web from the release paper first. Set the release paper aside, and use a nonstick appliqué pressing sheet (see page 9) or parchment paper on top of the web instead of the release paper. Press with a hot, dry iron for 7–10 seconds, and let the fabric cool before removing the pressing sheet.

● USING FAST2FUSE

The journal quilts in this book are all constructed on fast2fuse, a double-sided, fusible stiff interfacing (see Resources, page 63). Lightweight, yet firm, it may be used in place of, or with, batting. fast2fuse makes perfectly flat quilts, a desirable quality for the small wall quilt. fast2fuse is very stable and will not stretch, tear, or beard in use.

As with fusible web, store fast2fuse in a cool, dry place.

Quilts made with fast2fuse look crisp and finished. They can even have shaped or wavy edges rather than those boring old square edges (see *Fruit Flies,* page 34). But what's the best part of using fast2fuse for a small journal quilt? No rod pocket is needed! Quilts are lightweight, and a simple hanging loop is all you need to hang the quilt flat against the wall (see Display Options, page 59).

fast2fuse measures about 28" wide and comes rolled on a bolt to prevent creasing. It is also available in 14" × 18" Craft Packs. It cuts easily with scissors, rotary cutter blades, or craft knives. Mark it with a pencil or marker, or free-cut shapes without a pattern.

There is fusible glue on both sides of fast2fuse, so *release paper* or a *nonstick appliqué pressing sheet* must be placed beneath the product when ironing (see Pressing Aids, page 9). Do not allow a hot iron to touch the fast2fuse; the glue will melt onto the iron. To flatten fast2fuse for use, place it on release paper or a pressing sheet. Add another sheet of release paper on top, and iron for 5 seconds. After it cools, remove the release paper.

Fuse-tack fabric onto fast2fuse for about 5 seconds with a hot, dry iron. (Place release paper under the fast2fuse if there is no fabric on the other side.) Once the quilt composition is complete, steam set the glue for 10 seconds on each side of the fast2fuse for permanency. (Fusing directions come with the product.)

You can hand stitch through fast2fuse, but the better option is machine stitching. A sewing machine needle easily glides through fast2fuse. When you construct a fast2fuse quilt, the size of the quilt is limited by the width of the machine's stitching bed. fast2fuse quilts do not roll or fold like batted quilts. To make larger quilts with this product, join smaller units or panels of quilts with zigzag stitching like that in *A Division of Outer Space* (page 42).

Fusing Tools

● IRONS

Ideally you will have three irons for the construction of your fused journal quilts. (This explains why I have so many quilts about irons!) One iron is only for fusing fast2fuse and fusible web. It holds a steady, high heat (cotton setting) and is never used for steaming. (Steam hampers the initial transfer of fusible glue to fabric.) Steam holes on the sole plate do not interfere with the transfer of the glue.

A wand iron comes in handy for those tight corners and small elements found on journal quilts. Wand irons are lightweight and have a small surface plate and sharp points for reaching odd angles. I recommend the Clover Needlecraft Mini Iron.

Finally, you need a steam iron and a white cotton pressing cloth to steam set the glue after the fused composition is complete. Any good steam iron will work. Find one that has an even flow of steam and doesn't sputter or spew water. My favorite iron for steam setting is the Rowenta Expert Steam Generator, a heavy-duty iron with a large tank for water.

If you get fusible glue on the soleplate of your iron, remove it right away with an iron cleaner such as Dritz Iron Off. A hot, glue-covered iron will transfer the fusible glue to a quilt top, and once the glue is on fabric, it remains there permanently.

WAFFLE IRONS, 32″ × 37″, Laura Wasilowski

Pressing Aids

● RELEASE PAPER

Your most important pressing aid is release paper, which is the paper that fusible web comes on. After you transfer fusible web to fabric, the release paper no longer has glue on it. Keep the release paper in one piece when removing it from the fabric. Release paper carries a lubricant, allowing it to be fused to multiple times. Build fabric collages, construct component pieces, or store fused elements on the release paper; it will always release a fused fabric.

To protect your quilt top from glue on the iron, place a sheet of release paper on the quilt before ironing. If you are unsure which side of a fabric element holds the glue, fuse it between two pieces of release paper; the side that sticks to the release paper is the glue side. Release paper is also employed in a helpful pattern-transfer technique that I call *shape shifting* (used in *Perils of George*, page 28).

● NONSTICK PRESSING SHEET

A nonstick appliqué pressing sheet made of Teflon or other nonstick material also works for all the techniques mentioned above, except shape shifting. These nonstick sheets can be used repeatedly for collage building. If glue builds up on the surface of the sheet, remove the glue by scraping it off with a credit card or piece of stiff cardboard.

● IRONING SURFACE

To make your fusing days easier, find the largest ironing surface available. A cloth-covered surface keeps the iron cleaner than a metallic-coated surface. For workshops and classes, pack an ironing surface that is at least 18" wide.

It is important to keep the fusible web from sticking to the ironing surface or getting on the iron. Place release paper or a pressing sheet on the ironing surface for protection. Bear Thread Designs makes a 27" × 30" appliqué pressing sheet that works well (see Resources page 63).

CUTTING, PLACING, AND MARKING TOOLS

Sharp tools make a world of difference in the appearance of a fused journal quilt. The edges of design elements are not stitched, so a clean, crisp cut is best. Dull scissors or blades will rag and whisker fabric edges, detracting from the quilt's appearance. Keep three pairs of sharp scissors at hand: one for paper cutting, another for cutting large lengths of fabric and fast2fuse, and a small pair for snipping little fabric elements. For the small pair, select comfortable scissors with a sharp point. You will be using them frequently.

A standard 45mm rotary cutter, ruler, and cutting mat are part of your quilt construction arsenal. A fun addition is decorative rotary cutter blades. These blades (found in quilt shops and craft stores) come in wave, pinking, and scallop varieties and in other exotic shapes. They fit most 45mm diameter rotary cutters. When cutting with decorative blades, cut on the nongridded side of the mat, or the blade will mar the grid lines. Try to free-cut without a ruler; the blades will nick the edge of a ruler. Cut fused fabric with the **glue side up** to avoid tacking it to the mat and ragging the fabric when you lift it up.

Other tools to keep at hand are a pair of tweezers and a pencil or marker. Tweezers are essential for positioning those tiny elements that complete a fused journal quilt. You need a no. 2 pencil or a black Sharpie marker to mark the fast2fuse and for shape shifting (pages 11, 31).

SEWING TOOLS

Stitching through fast2fuse using a standard sewing machine is just like sewing through any other quilt filler. For handwork, stitch through fused fabrics and batting before attaching it to the fast2fuse. See Completing the Creation (pages 54–57) for complete information on quilting the fused journal quilt made with fast2fuse.

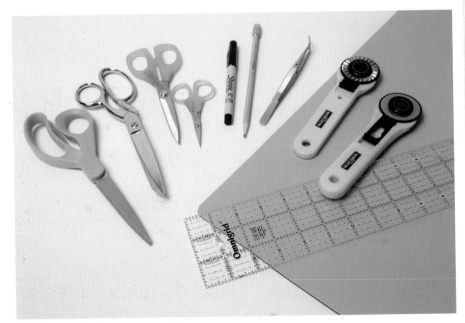

Tools for cutting, placing, and marking

CHICAGO SCHOOL OF FUSING POSTAGE, 9″ × 10″, Laura Wasilowski

FUSING QUICK REFERENCE GUIDE

The Chicago School of Fusing is not a real edifice; it is a state of mind. It is a belief that fusing provides flexible techniques to achieve glorious quilts. Many quilters have adopted fusible techniques as their favored form of expression.

Throughout this book, I mention many terms and techniques that are used in the fusing community. The following is a short list of those terms. For more information and a helpful guide to fused quilts, please read my book

Fusing Fun: Fast Fearless Art Quilts (C&T Publishing, 2005).

Free-cutting

Cut directly into the fabric without using a pattern or template or drawing on the fabric. Treat the fabric like a piece of paper, and draw the shape with your scissors or rotary cutter.

Fuse-tacking

Fuse the fabric elements for only 5 seconds; then remove the iron. Applying too much heat for too long will burn the fusible web into the fabric.

Overlapping/Underlapping

Join two fused fabrics by overlapping or underlapping the fabrics by about ¼″. Whenever possible, place the darker-value fabric on top of the lighter-value fabric to avoid a shadow caused by a darker fabric showing through a lighter fabric.

Shape Shifting

Use a black fine-point Sharpie marker or a no. 2 pencil to transfer a drawn shape to a fused fabric by tracing the pattern onto a piece of release paper. With the fabric glue side up, place the marked side of the release paper on the fabric. Fuse-tack for 5 seconds. Let the fabric cool, and then remove the paper. The pattern line will have transferred to the fabric, and you can follow that line to cut out the shape. You can also transfer a pencil line to the glue by placing the drawn line on the glue side of the fabric and rubbing the line with your fingertip. (See *Perils of George*, page 28.)

Steam Setting

Place a dry pressing cloth on top of the fabric to avoid iron marks. Apply a steam iron (cotton setting) by gliding the iron across the entire quilt, stopping for 10 seconds in each spot.

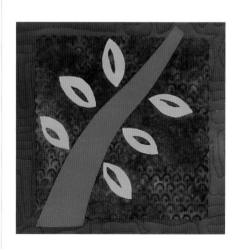

View from Above:
The Story of a Very Brave Woman

A Quick Nine-Patch Quilt

VIEW FROM ABOVE, 16″ × 16″, Laura Wasilowski

We bump down the grassy runway at the alarming speed of 75 mph. I'm strapped into the short little airplane, and my short little life flashes before me. Am I brave enough to ascend the heights? In the spirit of matrimonial harmony, I've acquired enough pluck to fly high above the earth with my husband in a small, two-seater airplane (built in 1949). If it weren't for the beautiful view, I'd risk the marriage and stay on the ground. But it's worth it. I am entranced by the colors and patterns of farm fields, orchards, and rolling grasslands that unfurl beneath me, reminding me of a patchwork quilt.

PRAIRIE BREEZE, 42″ × 48″, Laura Wasilowski
Doodles in a sketchbook can lead to quilt ideas.

INSPIRATION STRIKES!

View from Above documents in cloth my daring flight over the beautiful farmlands of southern Wisconsin. In the planted fields, wavy riverbanks, towering trees, and narrow country roads, I saw the basic elements of design: line, shape, color, and texture.

View from Above is a quick Nine-Patch quilt. Working directly with prefused fabrics, use fusing techniques such as free-cutting, fuse-tacking, overlapping, bias cutting, and a simple wrapped binding to make this quilt. These basic construction methods are easy to adapt to your own quilt designs. See Feeling Plucky? on how to convert your own daring experience into cloth.

FEELING PLUCKY?

Like flying, art making takes pluck. The brave artist is open to new ideas and looks for inspiration at every turn. Inspiration comes from many sources: experiences, nature, memories, photos, sketches, written documents, objects, animals, geometric shapes, even a conversation with a friend. Inspiration is everywhere!

To capture the visual essence of your inspiration, two things are required: observation and visualization. Observe the line, shape, color, and texture of your inspirational source. If you can't observe the source firsthand, try to visualize these items in your mind's eye. Distill the source of inspiration into the essential lines, shapes, colors, and textures that best describe it. These elements are in your own design language. They are personal symbols you create.

Sketchbook: Photos from flight

Your design information needs to be recorded, and a journal provides the perfect means to document your ideas. Call it your sketchbook, diary, notebook, or even memory bank. It is a place to hold these ideas so you can draw upon them and convert them into art. See Object of My Affection (page 20) for ideas about what to include in your journal.

BLUE FENCE, 40″ × 45″, Laura Wasilowski
Be inspired by memories of a favorite scene.

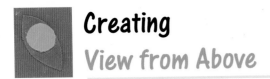

MATERIALS

- Field and tree fabrics: 10" × 10" each of 1 light green, 2 medium greens, 1 medium orange, 1 medium gold, and 1 medium brown
- Dark field fabrics: 4½" × 4½" each of 1 dark green, 1 dark orange, and 1 dark gold
- River fabric: 10" × 10" of medium turquoise
- Background fabric: 18" × 18" of medium blue
- Backing fabric: 16" × 16"
- Fusible web: 3¼" yards
- fast2fuse: 16" × 16"
- Machine quilting thread

Additional Tools

- Decorative rotary cutter blade, such as scallop, wave, or pinking
- Tweezers (optional)
- Nonstick pressing sheet (optional)

PREPARATION

1. Assemble all the materials and tools listed.

2. Iron fusible web to all the fabrics except the background fabric and backing fabric.

3. Remove the release paper from each fabric in one sheet. The squares in this quilt are constructed on the release paper, although a nonstick pressing sheet may be substituted for the release paper.

FIELD AND STREAM

1. Free-cut a square measuring about 4½" × 4½" from a corner of each field and tree fabric.

2. Use a rotary cutter with a decorative blade to trim all 4 sides of each square in Step 1 and each of the 3 dark field fabrics by about ¼" to make squares measuring about 4" × 4". These 9 squares are the bases for the 9 fields.

3. Place the larger light green field and tree fabric (with the square cut out) on the cutting mat, glue side up. Use a straight blade in the rotary cutter to cut the fabric diagonally from corner to corner as shown to form a large triangle. This cuts the fabric on the bias.

Tip ━━━━━━━━━━━━━━

The bias of fabric runs at 45° to the grain of the fabric. When fused, a bias-cut fabric will bend and wave easily to form curved lines.

4. Repeat Step 3 with the remaining field and tree fabrics.

Field Square 1

1. Place the trimmed 4″ × 4″ light green square on the release paper or pressing sheet, and fuse-tack in place.

2. Cut 3 bias strips measuring $\frac{1}{8}$″–$\frac{1}{4}$″ wide from the long bias side of each of the 2 medium green triangles. These strips are for the field stripes.

3. Place the end of a bias strip $\frac{1}{4}$″ beyond one corner of the light green square, and fuse-tack the end in place. Slowly curve and fuse-tack the strip across the square to the opposite corner. Trim the bias strip about $\frac{1}{4}$″ beyond the corner of the square.

4. Repeat Step 3 with the remaining bias strips, alternating the colors and leaving a span of about $\frac{1}{4}$″ between each strip. After the fabric cools, remove it from the release paper.

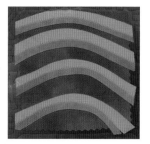

Field Square 2

1. Place the trimmed 4″ × 4″ dark green square on the release paper, and fuse-tack in place.

2. Cut 3 bias strips measuring $\frac{1}{4}$″–$\frac{1}{2}$″ wide from the long bias side of the medium orange triangle and a medium green triangle for a total of 6 bias strips.

3. Place the end of an orange bias strip $\frac{1}{4}$″ over the edge of the dark green square in the center. Fuse-tack the end in place. Slowly curve and fuse-tack the strip across the square. Trim the bias strip to within $\frac{1}{4}$″ of the outside edge.

4. Place a green bias strip just overlapping the edge of the orange strip, and fuse down the length of the orange strip. Trim to size.

5. Leaving a span of about $\frac{3}{4}$″ of dark green showing, place a second orange strip at the edge of the square. Repeat Steps 3 and 4 to fill the square. After the fabric cools, remove it from the release paper.

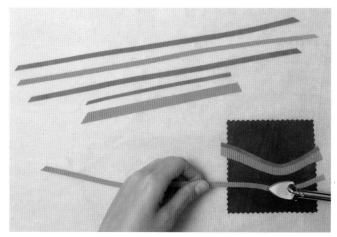

Field Square 3

1. Place the trimmed 4" × 4" medium gold square on release paper, and fuse-tack in place.

2. Cut 2 bias strips measuring about ½" wide from the long bias side of a medium green triangle. Free-cut 30 squares measuring about ½" × ½" from the bias strips.

3. Arrange the ½" squares on the gold square in a checker-board pattern, and fuse-tack in place. After the fabric cools, remove it from the release paper.

Field Square 4

1. Place a trimmed 4" × 4" medium green square on the release paper, and fuse-tack in place.

2. Cut a bias strip measuring about 1" wide from the long bias side of the brown triangle. Fold the strip in half, and cut to make 2 rectangular strips measuring 1" wide.

3. Cut across each brown strip diagonally from corner to corner to form 4 tapered triangular strips that measure about 1" wide at one end and that taper to ¹/₃₂" wide.

4. Place the narrow tips of the brown triangular strips about ¼" apart at the top left corner of the green square. Fan the wide ends of the strips across the square. Leave a span of green showing between each strip. Trim the bias strips to within ¼" of the outside edge of the square, and fuse-tack in place. After the fabric cools, remove it from the release paper.

Field Square 5

1. Place the other trimmed 4″ × 4″ medium green square on the release paper, and fuse-tack in place.

2. Cut 2 bias strips measuring about ¼″ wide from the long bias side of the light green and medium gold triangles for a total of 4 bias strips.

3. Cut the light green bias strips to size, and arrange them diagonally halfway across the green square. Leave a ½″ span of medium green showing between each strip, and fuse-tack in place.

4. Place a gold bias strip diagonally across the green square to cover the ends of the light green strips. Trim the strip to size, and add 2 more gold bias strips parallel to the first strip. Fuse-tack in place. After the fabric cools, remove it from the release paper.

River and Tree Blocks

1. Place the turquoise river fabric on the cutting mat. Cut the fabric square in half from one corner to the opposite corner on the bias to form 2 triangles. Cut 1 bias strip measuring about 1½″ wide from the long bias side of one triangle.

2. Fold this bias river strip in half, and cut to make 2 strips measuring about 1½″ wide. Cut across each strip from one corner to the opposite corner to form 4 tapered triangular strips that measure about 1¼″ wide and that taper to ¼″ wide.

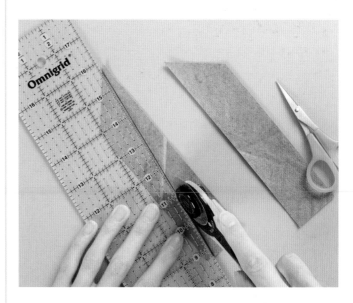

3. Place the trimmed 4″ × 4″ brown, dark gold, medium orange, and dark orange squares on release paper, and fuse-tack to hold them in place. One by one, place a river on each of the squares, fuse-tacking the narrow end of a bias river strip ¼″ over the edge of the square. Slowly curve and fuse-tack the strip across to the opposite side. Trim to within ¼″ of the outside edge of the square.

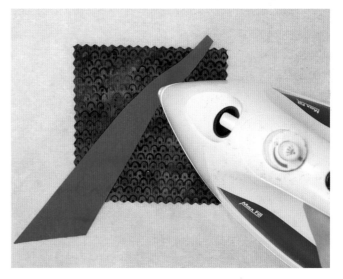

River and Tree Block 1

1. Free-cut 6 trees measuring about ¹/₂″ wide by 1″ long in a pointed oval shape from the medium gold.

2. Fold the gold ovals in half the long way, and cut out the centers. Place the trees on the riverbank of the brown square, and fuse-tack into place. After the fabric cools, remove it from the release paper.

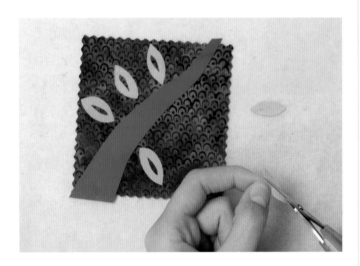

River and Tree Block 2

1. Free-cut 3 trees measuring about ¹/₂″ wide by 1″ long in a pointed oval shape from each of the medium greens. Place them on the riverbank of the dark orange square, and fuse-tack into place.

2. Free-cut 3 dots measuring about ¹/₄″ in diameter from the medium gold fabric. Place the dots on the green trees, and fuse-tack into place. After the fabric cools, remove it from the release paper.

River and Tree Block 3

1. Free-cut 3 trees measuring about ¹/₂″ wide by 1″ long in a pointed oval shape from the medium gold. Place them on the riverbank of the medium orange square, and fuse-tack into place.

2. Free-cut 2 trees measuring about ¹/₂″ wide by 1″ long in a pointed oval shape from the brown. Cut each tree in half the long way to form crescent shapes. Place a brown crescent on half of each gold tree, and fuse-tack into place. After the fabric cools, remove it from the release paper.

River and Tree Block 4

1. Free-cut 2 trees measuring about ½" wide by 1" long in a pointed oval shape from the light green and medium orange.

2. Cut the trees in half the long way to form crescent shapes. On the riverbank of the dark gold fabric, place 1 green and 1 orange crescent together to form a tree. Add 2 more green and orange trees. Fuse-tack into place. After the fabric cools, remove it from the release paper.

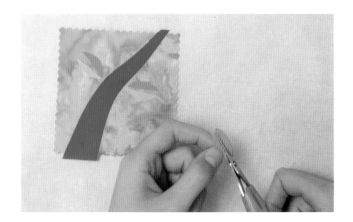

COMPLETING THE PROJECT

Refer to pages 54–60 for complete descriptions of quilting and finishing techniques.

1. Center and arrange the squares on the background fabric, leaving about 1" between each square. Fuse-tack in place.

2. Use Wrapped Binding #1 (page 57) to quilt and finish the quilt.

3. Add a hanging loop (page 59).

Object of My Affection: **Too Many Notions**

Building Fused Patterns to Make a Pincushion Quilt

OBJECT OF MY AFFECTION, 14″ × 16″, Laura Wasilowski

I am a collector of many notions and am especially fond of the sewing tools of my trade. My collection contains over 50 pairs of scissors, thimbles for all my fingers and toes, and more thread than a Wal-Mart warehouse. The current object of my affection is the pincushion. My pincushions appear in the form of chairs, chickens, even space ships. But it is the lowly tomato pincushion in my sewing toolbox that appeals to me the most.

INSPIRATION STRIKES!

A fondness for collecting inspired this quilt. Not only do I collect everyday objects related to sewing, but I also collect patterning ideas. Patterning is repeated motifs found on the surface of items like fabric, paper, pottery, buildings, anything with a decorated surface. Everyday objects and the patterning or surface design found on them are great sources of quilt design.

Object of My Affection is made by building patterned swatches of fabric with free-cut shapes. The swatches are then cut into shapes to form the object—a pincushion. Hand stitching adds another decorative layer of pattern to the surface of the quilt. To learn more about inspiring items to collect for your quilt design toolbox, see Collecting Inspiration.

COLLECTING INSPIRATION

Just like a pair of scissors or a pincushion, your journal is an important tool in the creation of your artwork. Your journal holds sketches, lists, notes, fabric swatches, and photos. It is like a toolbox full of ideas.

Sketchbook: Collection of patterning ideas

Adding to your quilt design toolbox is great fun. Collect items that personally inspire and appeal to you. Search for design triggers (see page 49 for more on design triggers) that capture your imagination and help create a quilt. Sketch, glue, tape, or even fuse the design ideas into your journal.

ELLY'S GARDEN #6, 8″ × 13″, Laura Wasilowski
Save cut-away fabrics from dot cutting to make even more patterns.

SEWING TOOL BOX, 19″ × 15″, Laura Wasilowski
Add pattern with batik fabrics in the border.

Creating
Object of My Affection

MATERIALS

- Wallpaper fabrics: 7″ × 9″ of 1 light blue and 1 light yellow
- Tablecloth fabric: 6″ × 11″ of medium yellow
- Tablecloth triangles fabric: 4″ × 7″ of medium blue
- Tomato pincushion and strawberry fabric: 4″ × 8″ of medium red-orange
- Pincushion dots fabric: 2″ × 9″ of medium blue
- Pincushion outline, tomato cap, and strawberry top fabric: 6″ × 9″ of medium green
- Pincushion and strawberry center dots fabric: 1″ × 2″ of medium yellow
- Border fabric: 13″ × 17″ of dark green
- Backing fabric: 14″ × 16″
- Fusible web: 1½ yards
- Batting: 12″ × 14″
- fast2fuse: 14″ × 16″
- Size 8 Pearl cotton embroidery thread in various colors
- Machine quilting thread

Additional Tools

- Decorative rotary cutter blade, such as scallop, wave, or pinking
- Embroidery needle for hand stitching
- Nonstick pressing sheet (optional)
- Tweezers (optional)

PREPARATION

1. Assemble all the materials and tools listed.

2. Iron fusible web to all the fabrics except the backing fabric.

3. Remove the release paper from each fabric in one sheet. Release paper will be needed for the construction of this quilt, although a nonstick pressing sheet may be substituted for the release paper.

FUSING THE PATTERNS
Wallpaper

1. Use a decorative blade in a rotary cutter to trim the edges of each wallpaper fabric by ½″ to make rectangles measuring about 6″ × 8″.

2. Use a decorative blade in a rotary cutter to free-cut 3 strips measuring about 2″ × 8″ from each of the wallpaper fabrics.

3. Place one of the wallpaper strips on release paper or a pressing sheet. Fuse-tack in place. Place a strip of the second wallpaper fabric on top of the long side of the first wallpaper strip, overlapping the first strip by about ¼″. Fuse-tack in place. Continue alternating the strips across to form the wallpaper background. After the fabric cools, remove it from the release paper.

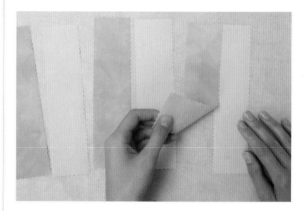

Tablecloth

1. Use a decorative blade to trim one of the long edges of the tablecloth fabric by ½″ to make a rectangle measuring about 5½″ × 11″.

2. Use a decorative blade to trim the tablecloth triangles fabric by ½" on all edges to make a rectangle measuring about 3" × 6". Free-cut this rectangle into 3 strips measuring about 1" × 6". Free-cut these strips into 18 squares measuring about 1" × 1".

3. Use a decorative blade to free-cut each square from Step 2 diagonally from corner to corner to form 2 triangles.

4. Place the tablecloth fabric on release paper (the decorative edge is the top of the tablecloth). Arrange the triangles from Step 3 on the tablecloth, and fuse-tack in place. After the fabric cools, remove it from the release paper.

Tomato Pincushion

1. Cut a rectangle measuring about 4" × 5" from the tomato pincushion fabric.

2. Cut 2 rectangles measuring about 1" × 9" from the pincushion dots fabric. Free-cut 9–10 dots measuring about ½" in diameter from each of the rectangles for a total of 18–20 dots.

3. Place the tomato pincushion fabric on release paper. Arrange the pincushion dots on the fabric. Fuse-tack in place. After the fabric cools, remove it from the release paper.

4. Fold the tomato pincushion fabric in half, fused side out, so the short sides are together. Holding the folded edge, free-cut a long rounded arc as shown. The cut fabric should resemble a long rounded oval when opened.

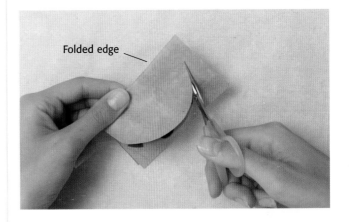

Folded edge

5. Keep the piece folded in half, and free-cut a shallow arc as shown to form the left and right sections of the tomato.

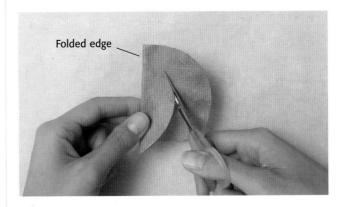

Folded edge

6. Free-cut a rectangle measuring about 5" × 6" from the pincushion outline fabric. Fuse-tack to the release paper.

7. Center the tomato sections on the outline fabric. Separate the sections by about ⅛" to reveal the green outline fabric underneath. Fuse-tack in place. After the fabric cools, remove it from the release paper.

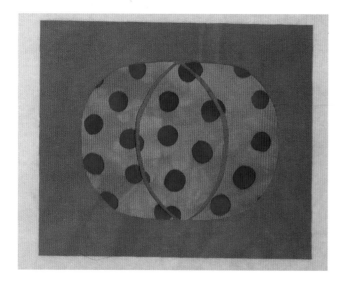

8. Trim the outline fabric to within ⅛" of the exterior of the tomato shape.

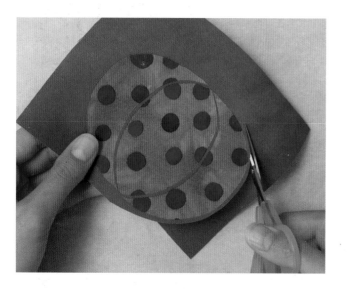

9. Cut a rectangle measuring about 1½" × 6" from the tomato cap fabric. Center the tomato on top of the long side of the tomato cap fabric, leaving about ¼" of the fabric showing on top. Using the edge of the tomato as a guide, trim the tomato cap fabric around the tomato's arc. Remove the tomato, and set it aside.

10. Free-cut 3 shallow arcs from the long straight edge of the tomato cap to form the tomato cap leaves.

11. Place the tomato on release paper. Arrange the tomato cap on the top of the tomato. Fuse-tack in place.

Strawberry

1. Cut a square measuring about 2" × 2" from the strawberry fabric. Starting at a corner, free-cut a rounded triangle from the square. Trim a small arc from each side of the triangle to form a strawberry shape.

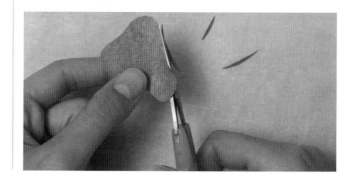

2. Cut a rectangle measuring about 1″ × 2″ from the strawberry top fabric. Repeat the directions for cutting and fusing in Steps 9–11 for the tomato to fit the strawberry top to the strawberry.

3. Free-cut 2 dots measuring about ½″ in diameter from the pincushion and strawberry center dots fabric. Place the pincushion and strawberry on release paper. Center the dots on the tops of the pincushion and strawberry. Fuse-tack in place. After the fabric cools, remove it from the release paper.

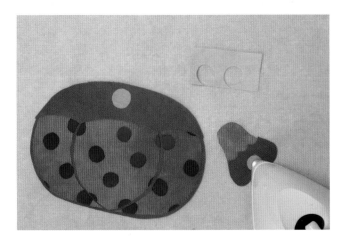

ASSEMBLING THE COLLECTION

1. Orient the batting vertically with the scrim side down (see page 54 for batting information). Place the wallpaper fabric (with the stripes running vertically) on the top portion of the batting. Fuse-tack in place.

2. Center the decorative edge of the tablecloth fabric on the lower edge of the wallpaper fabric, overlapping the wallpaper by about ¼″. Fuse-tack in place.

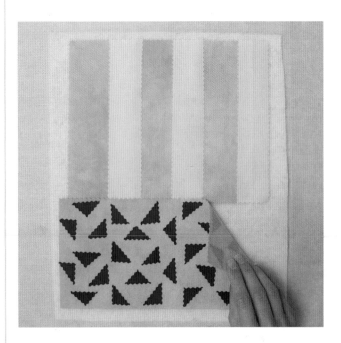

3. Arrange the tomato and strawberry on the background. Fuse-tack in place.

4. Steam set (page 11) the quilt top to the batting. Trim away excess batting.

5. Using the photo of *Object of My Affection* (page 20) as a guide, add hand stitches to the quilt top through the batting. With the size 8 Pearl cotton thread, connect the tomato and strawberry with an embroidered backstitch. Add the seed stitch on the strawberry, running stitch on the tomato cap, running and lazy daisy stitches on the wallpaper, and cross-stitches on the tablecloth. (See Resources, page 63, for books on embroidery.)

6. Use a decorative blade to cut 2 strips measuring about 3″ × 13″ and 2 strips measuring about 3″ × 17″ from the border fabric.

7. Place the quilt top on release paper.

8. Center the decorative edge of a 13″ border strip on top of the left side of the quilt, overlapping the quilt by ¼″. Fuse-tack in place.

9. Repeat Step 8 on the right side of the quilt.

10. Center a 17″ border strip on top of the top edge of the quilt and side borders, overlapping the edge by ¼″. Fuse-tack in place.

11. Repeat Step 10 on the bottom edge of the quilt. After the fabric cools, remove the quilt top from the release paper.

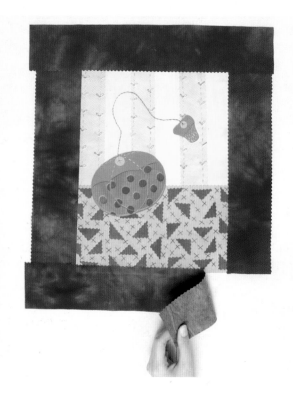

COMPLETING THE PROJECT

Refer to pages 54–60 for complete descriptions of quilting and finishing techniques.

1. Use Wrapped Binding #1 (page 57) to quilt and finish the quilt.

2. Add a hanging loop (page 59).

Perils of George: **A Very Bad Dog**

An Easy Quilt Adapted from a Sketch

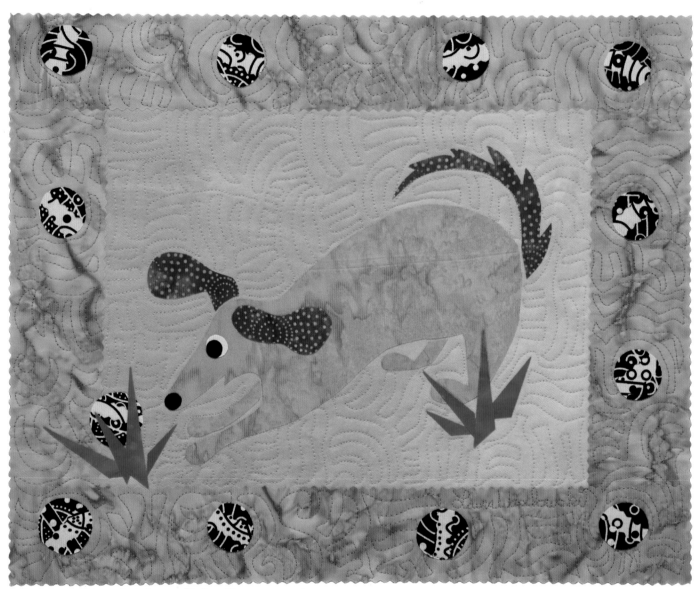

PERILS OF GEORGE, 15″ × 12″, Laura Wasilowski

George the dog is like the James Bond of the canine world. His life is fraught with constant danger and adventure. Every day my friend Frieda Anderson walks George through the woods, and every day a new **Perils of George** story unfolds.

One day George surprises his arch enemy, the neighborhood skunk, in the backyard. After a thorough spraying with skunk juice, George races into the house, leaps into Frieda's bed, and hides under the covers. George is a very bad dog, but Frieda loves him anyway.

CURIOUS GEORGE, 12" × 15", Laura Wasilowski
A sketch defines the shapes and placement of the objects in the story.

INSPIRATION STRIKES!

Stories about George and his crazy antics inspired my series of patterns depicting his many adventures. The stories, recorded in my sketchbook, are easy to convert into patterns because they are filled with action—George running, digging, or barking up a tree. I began with quick sketches of the exploits of a cartoon-like dog. After I refined and enlarged the sketches, the *Bad Dog* patterns were born.

George may be a handful, but this quilt is quite simple and easy. *Perils of George* is made with a quick pattern-transfer technique I call *shape shifting* (page 11). In shape shifting, the pattern lines are traced onto release paper and transferred to a fused fabric with a hot iron. For hints on how this method of pattern transfer can be used with other pattern sources to make up your own story, see Stories in Cloth.

STORIES IN CLOTH

Stories, especially humorous ones, are a constant source of quilt inspiration for me. Much like a children's book or nursery rhyme, the story quilt needs two items: a subject and an action. The subject of the story, whether animal, vegetable, or object, is seen doing something (running, tilting, singing, playing the banjo, resting). Try to encapsulate the tale into

one exploit that best describes the action taking place.

To capture the essence of your story, consider using a sketch for reference. A sketch helps define the shapes and placement of the objects in the story. For an example of how a sketch is converted into a pattern, see *Fruit Flies* (page 34).

Sketchbook: George in action

Another option is to use patterns with simple, enclosed shapes, like appliqué patterns. Enlargements of images in the public domain can also be converted into patterns. By adjusting the scale on a copy machine, you can combine patterns from different sources in one quilt to tell your story. Always make sure you have permission to use a design source before adapting it to a pattern, or I'll send George to your house.

HAPPY DOG, 12" × 15", Laura Wasilowski
Animate the subject of your quilt—imply action.

Creating
Perils of George

MATERIALS

- Background fabric: 9″ × 12″ of light value
- Dog body fabric: 8″ × 10″ of medium value
- Dog ears and tail fabric: 4″ × 8″ of medium value
- White eye fabric: 1″ × 1″ of white
- Black eye and nose fabric: 1″ × 2″ of black
- White ball fabric: 3″ × 7″ of white with some black print on top
- Black ball fabric: 4½″ × 7″ black with some white print on top
- Grass fabric: 2″ × 2″ medium green
- Border fabric: 10″ × 16″ of medium value
- Backing fabric: 13″ × 16″
- Fusible web: 1½ yards
- fast2fuse: 13″ × 16″
- Machine quilting thread

Additional Tools

- Decorative rotary cutter blade, such as scallop, wave, or pinking
- Black fine-point Sharpie marker or no. 2 pencil
- Nonstick pressing sheet (optional)

PREPARATION

1. Assemble all the materials and tools listed.

2. Iron fusible web to all the fabrics except the backing and background fabrics.

3. Remove the release paper from each fabric in one sheet. Release paper will be needed for the construction of the quilt and the pattern-transfer process.

A DOG'S LIFE

Background and Borders

1. Place the fast2fuse on release paper or a nonstick pressing sheet. Center the backing fabric on the fast2fuse, and fuse-tack in place. After the fabric cools, remove the release paper. Turn the piece over so the fast2fuse side is facing up.

2. Center the background fabric horizontally on top of the fast2fuse. About 2″ of fast2fuse will frame the background fabric. Place release paper on top of the fast2fuse, and fuse-tack the fabric in place. After the fabric cools, remove the release paper.

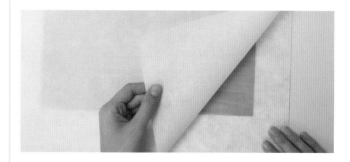

3. Use a rotary cutter with a decorative blade to cut out 2 strips of border fabric to measure about 2¼″ × 9″ and 2 more border strips to measure about 2¼″ × 16″.

4. Center a 9″ border strip on the left-hand side of the background fabric, overlapping the background fabric by ¼″. Fuse-tack in place. Repeat on the right side of the background fabric with the second 9″ strip.

5. Center a 16″ border strip on the top edge of the background fabric and side border strips, overlapping the background fabric by ¼″. Fuse-tack in place. Repeat on the bottom edge of the background fabric with the second 16″ strip.

George

1. Place the release paper on the dog body pattern (page 61). Trace the pattern with a Sharpie marker or a no. 2 pencil, and remove the release paper.

2. Place the marked side of the release paper on the glue side of the dog fabric. Fuse the paper in place for 5 seconds. Let the fabric cool.

3. Carefully remove the release paper from the fabric. The ink will have transferred to the glue. (This is shape shifting.)

4. Use scissors to cut out the shape just inside the black line.

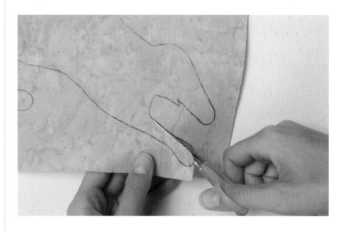

5. Repeat Steps 1–4 for the dog's right front paw and right rear paw (using the remaining dog body fabric) and the dog's ears and tail (using the ear and tail fabric).

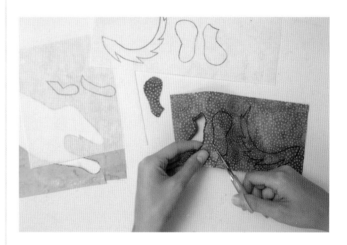

6. Center the dog body on the lower part of the background fabric. Fuse-tack in place.

7. Place the dog paws, top ear, and tail about ¹⁄₁₆″ from where they join the dog's body. Fuse-tack in place. Add the bottom ear on top of the dog's head, and fuse-tack in place.

8. Free-cut a dot measuring about ½" in diameter from the white eye fabric. Free-cut 2 dots measuring about ⅜" in diameter from the black eye and nose fabric.

9. Place the white eye dot on the dog's head, and position the black eye dot on top of the white dot. Fuse-tack in place. Place the nose on the tip of the dog's snout. Fuse-tack in place.

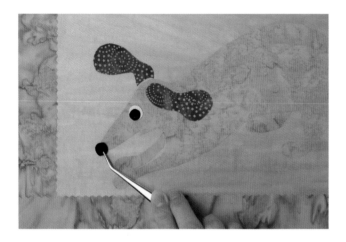

Balls

1. Cut the white ball fabric into 3 strips measuring about 1" × 7". Use a decorative blade to free-cut the black ball fabric into 6 strips measuring about ¾" × 7".

2. Place a white strip on release paper, and fuse-tack in place. Center the decorative edge of a black strip on top of the long side of the white strip, overlapping the white strip by about ¼". Fuse-tack in place.

3. Repeat Step 2 on the other side of the white strip. After the fabric cools, remove it from the release paper.

4. Repeat Steps 2–3 for the remaining 2 white strips and 4 black strips.

5. Free-cut 12 dots measuring about 1" in diameter from the black and white strips.

6. Place a ball near the dog's nose, and fuse-tack in place. Place the remaining 11 balls around the border of the quilt. Fuse-tack in place.

Grass

1. Cut the grass fabric square diagonally from corner to corner to form 2 triangles.

2. Cut 2 bias strips each measuring about ½" wide from the long bias side of each of the grass triangles for a total of 4 bias strips.

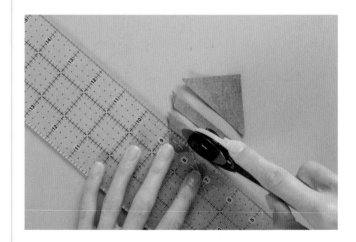

3. Cut across each grass bias strip diagonally from corner to corner to form tapered triangular strips that measure $\frac{1}{2}''$ wide at one end and that taper to about $\frac{1}{32}''$ wide for a total of 8 blades of grass.

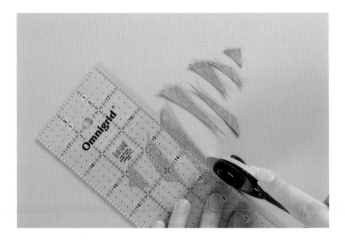

4. Arrange the blades of grass on top of the ball, dog, and border. Fuse-tack in place.

Refer to pages 54–60 for complete descriptions of quilting and finishing techniques.

1. Use Trimmed Binding (page 57) to quilt and finish the quilt.

2. Add a hanging loop (page 59).

Fruit Flies:
A Story Told Around the Kitchen Table

Making Unique Surface Textures

FRUIT FLIES III, 15″ × 15″, Laura Wasilowski

We have pets at our house, very tiny pets. We have fruit flies.
Colony after colony of little fruit flies grow from baby fly to
elder fly in our kitchen. There have been so many flies that we
no longer name them. Here they are, taking their lunch out
for a picnic on the kitchen table. It's good to have pets.

WAITING FOR WEEZIE, 38″ × 30″, Laura Wasilowski
Enlarge and convert a sketch into fabric elements.

INSPIRATION STRIKES!

Clever remarks, puns, or wordplay are always jotted down with a chortle and a grin. This quilt was inspired by the note "fruit flies" on my journal page. That led to a quick sketch, which led to the quilt and the story about my "pets."

In *Fruit Flies,* exciting surface-texturing devices like fabric folding, fused weaving, and fused trapunto lift the quilt into the third dimension. (I've given you the pattern for the quilt, but to learn more about converting a sketch into a pattern, see Sketchy Information.) May these innovative fusing techniques add to your fusing repertoire and give you as much pleasure as my little pets have given me.

SKETCHY INFORMATION

For most artists, a sketch is the warm-up for the main act, a way to work out the composition before committing it to fabric. The quilt sketch for *Fruit Flies* acts as a diagram. It gives this basic information: size, shape, and arrangement of shapes in the composition. Like a cartoon or a page from a coloring book, sketches for quilts must have enclosed shapes. These enclosed shapes are converted into patterns, or templates, that then become fabric shapes.

Converting a Sketch into Pattern

Use a copy machine or computer scanner to convert a sketch into a pattern as follows:

1. Make a clean tracing of the sketch using tracing paper or release paper. If you can't see the sketch through the paper, use a lightbox, or place the sketch and paper on a window.

2. As you trace, simplify the lines, and make enclosed shapes. Enclosed shapes have lines all around their edges, like the shapes in a coloring book. Fine details of the sketch need not be drawn. You can add these details later by applying free-cut fabric shapes or stitching.

Sketchbook: Fruit Flies sketches

3. Enlarge the refined sketch to the desired size at your local copy store. Or scan the sketch into your computer, enlarge it to the size desired, and print out the pattern.

4. Use the shape-shifting technique of pattern transfer (pages 11, 31) to convert your pattern into fabric elements.

COLORADO MOON, 17″ × 20″, Laura Wasilowski
Add texture to the quilt surface with colored cheesecloth.

Creating
Fruit Flies

MATERIALS

- Table fabric: 6″ × 14″ of light value
- Cheesecloth: 9″ × 14″ painted or dyed a medium value
- Wall fabric: 9″ × 14″ of light value
- Bowl fabrics: 6″ × 10″ each of 2 complementary dark values
- Oranges fabric: 4″ × 7″ of orange
- Other fruit fabrics: 5″ × 5″ each of apple red, pear green, and grape purple
- Stem fabric: 2″ × 2″ of brown
- Backing fabric: 18″ × 18″
- Fusible web: 2 yards
- Batting: 8″ × 8″
- fast2fuse: 15″ × 15″
- Hand (optional) and machine quilting thread

Additional Tools

- Decorative rotary cutter blade, such as scallop wave, or pinking
- Black fine-point Sharpie marker or no. 2 pencil
- Tweezers (optional)
- Hand embroidery needle for hand stitching (optional)
- Nonstick pressing sheet (optional)

Tip

White cotton cheesecloth can be dyed like any other cotton fabric or painted with water-based textile paints. To paint, thin the paint to a water-color consistency, place the fabric on a plastic sheet, and paint with a sponge brush. Fuse the fabric after it is completely dry.

PREPARATION

1. Assemble all the materials and tools listed.

2. Iron fusible web to all the fabrics except the backing fabric. Place release paper or a pressing sheet beneath the cheesecloth when fusing to protect the ironing surface from the glue.

Note: Always protect the iron by covering the cheese-cloth with release paper or a pressing sheet when ironing. Eventually the glue from the gaps in the cheesecloth will burn off and no longer stick to the iron.

3. Remove the release paper from each fabric, except the table fabric, in one sheet. Release paper will be needed for the construction of this quilt, although a nonstick pressing sheet may be substituted for the release paper.

ADDING FIBER TO YOUR LIFE
Table

1. Place the cheesecloth, glue side down, on top of the table fabric. (The table fabric still has the release paper on the back.) Hand pleat the cheesecloth into horizontal folds so it fits across the table fabric. The folds do not have to be even or exactly sized. Place release paper or a pressing sheet on top of the cheesecloth, and press the folds in place.

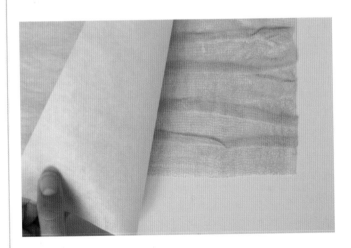

2. After the fabric cools, remove the release paper from the back and front of the cheesecloth/table fabric. Use a decorative blade to trim about ¼″ from one of the long sides of the table fabric.

3. Place the wall fabric horizontally on release paper or a pressing sheet. Fuse-tack in place.

4. Center the decorative edge of the cheesecloth/table fabric on the lower edge of the wall fabric, overlapping the wall fabric edge about ¼". Place a piece of release paper on the cheesecloth/table fabric, and fuse-tack into place. After the fabric cools, remove the release paper from the cheesecloth/table fabric.

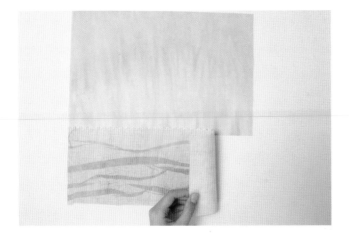

3. Carefully remove the release paper from the fabric. The ink will have transferred to the glue. (This is shape shifting.)

4. Use scissors to cut out the shape just inside the black line.

Bowl

1. Place release paper on the bowl pattern (page 62). Trace the pattern with a Sharpie marker or a no. 2 pencil, and remove the release paper.

2. Place the marked side of the release paper on the glue side of one of the bowl fabrics. Fuse the paper in place for 5 seconds. Let the fabric cool.

5. Repeat Steps 1–4 for the other bowl fabric.

6. Place a bowl, glue side up, on the cutting mat. Free-cut 5 strips measuring about ³⁄₄″ wide **horizontally** across the fabric. Follow the gentle arc of the bowl's top curve. Place the horizontal strips in order, glue side down, on release paper. **Lightly** fuse-tack the left half of the bowl.

7. Place the remaining bowl fabric on the cutting mat. Free-cut strips measuring about ³⁄₄″ wide **vertically** through the fabric. Curve the cuts slightly to match the arcs of the bowl's sides.

8. Weave the right-hand vertical strip in through the right-hand side of the horizontal bowl strips. Go under the top horizontal strip, over the next strip, under the next strip, and so on, following the curved edges of the bowl. Use the tip of pointed scissors to align all the edges into the bowl shape. **Lightly** fuse-tack the strip in place.

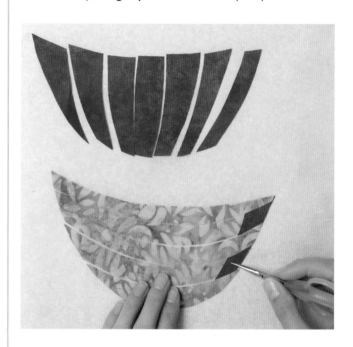

9. From the left-hand side, carefully lift the horizontal strips from the release paper up to the first vertical strip. Weave the next vertical strip to the left of the first one. This time go over the top strip, under the next strip, and so on. Use the tip of the scissors to snug the strip up closely to the first vertical strip. Align the top and bottom of the strip with the horizontal strips. Lightly fuse-tack in place.

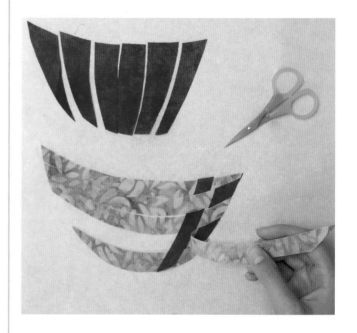

10. Continue weaving the vertical strips in order across the bowl to the left. Align the top and bottom of each strip with the horizontal strips. Lightly fuse-tack each strip.

11. After the fabric cools, carefully remove the bowl from the release paper. Trim the edges to shape.

Fruit

1. Free-cut 2 large circles measuring about 2½″ in diameter from the oranges fabric to make the oranges.

2. Using the shape-shifting method described in Steps 1–4 for the bowl, transfer the apple and pear patterns (page 62) to make the apple and pear; or free-cut each shape.

3. Free-cut 5 strips measuring about 1″ × 5″ from the grapes fabric. Free-cut 15 grape dots measuring about ¾″ in diameter from the grape strips.

4. Place a grape on release paper. Overlap additional grapes to form a triangular cluster of grapes. Fuse-tack in place.

5. Cut the batting into 4 squares each measuring about 4″ × 4″. Place the cut orange fabric on a batting square, and cut the batting to the shape. Remove the orange fabric, and trim ¼″ around the batting to make it smaller than the orange fabric.

6. Place the orange-shaped batting on release paper. Center the orange on top of the batting, and fuse-tack in place. After the fabric cools, remove it from the release paper.

7. Repeat Steps 5–6 for the other orange and for the apple and pear.

8. If you like, add hand stitching such as seed stitch, French knots, or cross-stitches to the oranges, apple, and pear shapes. (See Resources, page 63, for books on embroidery.)

9. Free-cut 3 stems measuring about ¼" × 1" from the stem fabric for the apple, pear, and grapes. While cutting, curve the long sides of the stems, and round one end of the stem (you will place this end on the fruit). Free-cut 2 small ovals measuring about ¼" × ½" from the stem fabric for the 2 orange stems.

Arranging the Fruit

1. Position the bowl, fruit, and stems on the wall and table. Tuck the pear just under the top rim of the bowl. Cover the cheesecloth/table area with release paper. Fuse-tack everything in place.

2. After the fabric cools, remove it from the release paper.

COMPLETING THE PROJECT

Refer to pages 54–60 for complete descriptions of quilting and finishing techniques.

1. Place the fast2fuse on the cutting mat. Starting about 2″ in from each corner, trim the fast2fuse edges by about ¼″. Cut shallow waves and arcs with a rotary cutter. For more stability use a ruler to hold the fast2fuse in place while cutting.

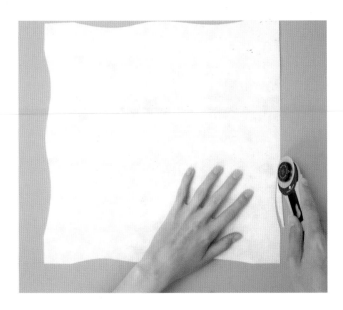

2. Use Wrapped Binding #2 (page 58) to quilt and finish the quilt.

3. Add a hanging loop (page 59).

A Division of Outer Space

An Abstract Quilt Constructed in Panels

A DIVISION OF OUTER SPACE, 18" × 24", Laura Wasilowski

We are at the opening of the Chicago School of Fusing Faculty Exhibit at the Fermilab Gallery near Batavia, Illinois. Emily Parson, my fellow exhibitor, engages a resident nuclear physicist in conversation. The man is explaining the mission of Fermilab: to smash atoms and study the minute particles that result. After his lengthy and in-depth explanation, Emily says, "Oh, so it's like...science."

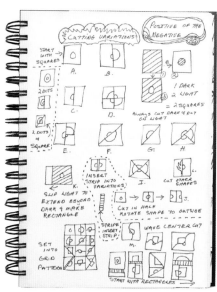

Sketchbook: Planning *A Division of Outer Space*

INSPIRATION STRIKES!

This inspiring story illustrates the close relationship between fusers and physicists. Both dismantle things, arrange the elements to their satisfaction, and try to make sense of it all. Quiltmakers are the nuclear physicists of the art world.

came to a frightening conclusion: There are an infinite number of color combinations, an infinite number of ways to cut the squares, and an infinite number of ways to reassemble them. The task appeared daunting until I turned to my sketchbook for help.

By drawing and writing about construction variations, I record all of my ideas in one place. Ideas are compared, and technical questions are answered. My notes help me to work out the possibilities, to explore the many options before actually committing them to fabric.

In *A Division of Outer Space*, both positive and negative shapes are made from fabric squares. The squares are divided, reassembled into new units, adhered to separate fast2fuse panels, and combined to make an abstract quilt. Don't worry; although this is an improvisational method of quilt composition, it's not like…science.

THE BIG BANG THEORY OF QUILTING

Like the vastness of the universe, fusing presents endless possibilities. When designing *A Division of Outer Space*, I

PRINCESS LOUISE POPPIES #1, 11″ × 10″, Laura Wasilowski Offset panels to add interest.

CHERRY ORCHARD, 15″ × 6½″, Laura Wasilowski Stitches between fast2fuse panels act as hinges for this desktop quilt.

MATERIALS

- Quilt top fabrics: 16″ × 16″ each of 3 medium values
- Dark squares fabrics: 6″ × 10″ each of 3 dark values
- Light squares fabrics: 10″ × 10″ each of 3 light values
- Insert fabric: 4″ × 4″ of bright highlight
- Backing fabric: 18″ × 24″
- fast2fuse: 18″ × 24″
- Fusible web: 3½ yards
- Machine quilting thread

Additional Tools

- Nonstick pressing sheet (optional)

PREPARATION

1. Assemble all the materials and tools listed.

2. Iron fusible web to all the fabrics except the quilt top fabrics.

3. Remove the release paper from each fabric in one sheet. The squares in this quilt are constructed on the release paper, although a nonstick pressing sheet may be substituted for the release paper.

THE POSITIVE OF THE NEGATIVE

Make Light and Dark Squares

1. Cut 4 squares measuring 8″ × 8″ from each of the 3 unfused quilt top fabrics.

2. Cut 12 squares measuring 6″ × 6″ from the fast2fuse.

3. Center a fast2fuse square on the wrong side of a quilt top square. Turn the quilt top and fast2fuse over, keeping everything in place. Place the fast2fuse on release paper or a pressing sheet. Fuse-tack the quilt top to the fast2fuse. After the fabric cools, remove it from the release paper.

4. Repeat Step 3 with the remaining 11 squares of quilt top fabrics and fast2fuse.

5. Follow Steps 4–8 of Wrapped Binding #1 (page 57) to bind each square.

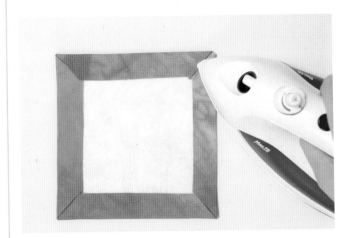

6. Cut 12 squares measuring about 5½″ × 5½″ from the quilt backing fabric.

7. Center a backing fabric square on the back of each fast2fuse square. Fuse-tack in place.

8. Cut 2 squares measuring 4″ × 4″ from each of the dark squares fabrics.

9. Cut 4 squares measuring 4″ × 4″ from each of the light squares fabrics.

10. Fold a dark square in half with the glue side out.

11. Starting on the fold about 1″ up from the bottom edge of the square, use scissors to free-cut a semicircle with a 1″ radius from the center of the square.

Folded edge —

12. Place a light square on release paper or a pressing sheet. Center the dark square from Step 11 (with the hole cut from the center) on the light square. Fuse-tack in place. After the fabric cools, remove it from the release paper. This creates a dark fused square.

13. Place a light square on release paper. Center the small circle cut out in Step 11 on the square, and fuse-tack in place. After the fabric cools, remove it from the release paper. This creates a light fused square.

14. Repeat Steps 10–13 with the remaining 5 dark squares. **Always cut shapes from the dark squares. Do not cut the light squares.** Vary the shapes of the cutouts, making rounded squares and triangles, pointed ovals, eggs, or other symmetric shapes.

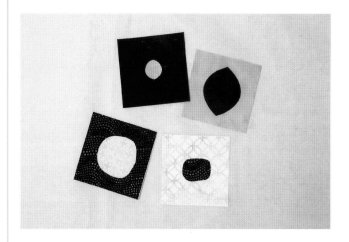

Cut and Reassemble the Squares

1. Set aside 2 light fused squares and 1 dark fused square. These will remain whole.

2. Select 1 light fused square and 1 dark fused square. Cut both squares diagonally from corner to corner to form 4 triangles total.

3. Place a light triangle from Step 2 on release paper. Place the long side of a dark triangle on top of the long side of the light triangle, overlapping the light triangle by ¼", to form a square. Fuse-tack in place. Repeat for the remaining pair of triangles. After the fabric cools, remove it from the release paper.

4. Cut the remaining 7 fused squares in half through the center to form 14 rectangles total.

5. Place a light rectangle on release paper. Place the long side of a dark rectangle on top of the long side of the light rectangle, overlapping the light rectangle by about ¼", to form a square. Fuse-tack in place. After the fabric cools, remove it from the release paper.

6. Repeat Step 5 with 3 more light and 3 more dark rectangles to form 3 more squares.

7. Cut 3 strips each measuring 1" × 4" from the insert fabric.

8. Place an insert strip on release paper. Center the long side of a light rectangle on top of the insert strip, overlapping the insert strip by ¼". Center the long side of a dark rectangle on top of the other side of the insert fabric, overlapping by ¼". Fuse-tack in place. After the fabric cools, remove it from the release paper.

9. Repeat Step 8 with the remaining light and dark rectangles and insert fabric strips. Note: One set of the rectangles will contain **2 dark** rectangles.

10. If any squares have fabrics from underneath showing, trim the underneath fabric so it doesn't show.

FUSION IT ALL TOGETHER

1. Place the fast2fuse squares made with the quilt top fabrics, right side up, in 3 adjoining vertical rows of 4 squares each.

2. Place a decorated square on each of the fast2fuse squares. Arrange and rearrange the squares until the composition feels balanced. Offset or tilt some of the squares to add interest. Fuse-tack in place.

3. Steam set the front and back of each fast2fuse square.

4. Abut the top left fast2fuse square against the square beneath it in that vertical row. Use a wide zigzag or similar decorative stitch to join the 2 squares by stitching down the center of the join.

5. Repeat Step 4, adding the next square in that vertical row and the final square in that row.

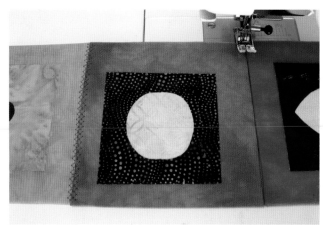

6. Repeat Steps 4 and 5 for the next 2 vertical rows.

7. Abut the left vertical row of squares against the center vertical row of squares. Use a wide zigzag or similar decorative stitch to join the 2 rows by stitching down the center of the join.

8. Add the final vertical row as described in Step 7.

9. Add 3 hanging loops (page 59) to the back of the quilt.

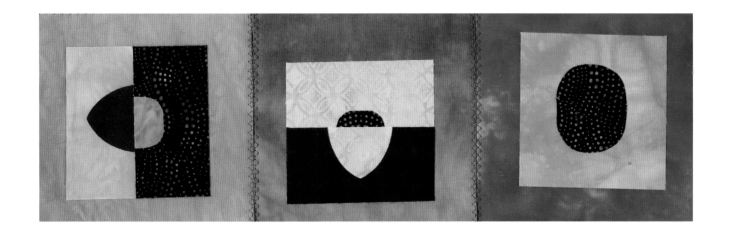

Peaceful Landscape:
A Deceptively Calm Day

Improvising with Fused Fabrics

PEACEFUL LANDSCAPE, 16″ × 16″, Laura Wasilowski

Disaster follows me like a lonely dog. In my teaching travels, I encounter blinding snowstorms, freezing rain, and in one case, a citywide power outage while I was teaching fusing. But I wasn't expecting this next disaster: As I walked down the street, I turned and saw my house flying through the air! Then I remembered that I had forgotten to pay the gravity bill.

INSPIRATION STRIKES!

The house story isn't true, but *Peaceful Landscape* was inspired by real-life events. While sorting out scraps of fused fabric, I came across a length of silk with a frayed edge. The scrap reminded me of reeds in a swamp, and a quilt idea was born. When I was midway through designing the landscape, fabric resembling a house fell onto the sky portion of the landscape. Seeing this, my son, Gus, said, "Hey, Mom. Did you forget to pay the gravity bill?"

Serendipity is a beautiful thing. The design and story of *Peaceful Landscape* were discovered by chance, and the quilt is constructed through improvisation. Improvisational quiltmaking leads to more ideas and to the expansion of your creative experience. To learn more about how to add improvisational quilt designs to your repertoire, see Design Triggers.

PRODUCE DEPARTMENT #3, 17″ × 18″, Laura Wasilowski
Cut the random acts of fusing into a specific shape

DESIGN TRIGGERS

There are days when disaster strikes my creative abilities as well. A solution is to play with fused fabric scraps left over from other projects. The serendipitous shapes suggest images that are not always found in my sketchbook or journal. Improvising with these design triggers has inspired many new quilt designs.

Fused confetti can also be used to build *random acts of fusing*. Randomly overlap and fuse the fabric scraps onto a piece of release paper. Build the collage into a specific shape, or cut it into shape after removing it from the release paper. Fused fabric scraps also make great collages for the back of your fast2fuse quilts.

PEACEFUL LANDSCAPE (back), 16″ × 16″, Laura Wasilowski
Back the quilt with random acts of fusing.

Creating
Peaceful Landscape

MATERIALS

- Sky fabric: 5″ × 12″ of pastel pink
- Water fabric: 3″ × 11″ of pastel blue
- Wheat field fabric: 2″ × 5″ of deep gold
- Tree line fabric: 1½″ × 13″ of purple
- Swamp fabric: 5″ × 12″ of green
- Reeds fabric: 2″ × 9″ of rust dupioni or other silk
- Front field fabric: 2″ × 12″ of medium gold
- Grass fabric: 3″ × 3″ of orange
- House fabric: 2″ × 3½″ of green
- Architectural features fabrics: 2″ × 2″ each of blue, orange, and gold
- Background fabric: 18″ × 18″ of pastel blue
- Backing fabric: 16″ × 16″
- Fusible web: 1 yard
- Batting: 16″ × 16″
- fast2fuse: 16″ × 16″

Additional Tools

- Decorative rotary cutter blade, such as scallop, wave, or pinking
- Straight pin or T-pin
- Tweezers (optional)
- Nonstick pressing sheet (optional)

PREPARATION

1. Assemble all the materials and tools listed.

2. Iron fusible web to all the fabrics except the swamp, reeds, front field, background, and backing fabrics.

3. Remove the release paper from each fabric in one sheet. The release paper will be needed for the construction of this quilt, although a nonstick pressing sheet may be substituted for the release paper.

SWAMP LANDS

1. Use a decorative blade to free-cut a shallow, convex arc from one long side of the sky fabric. In a similar manner, trim the 2 short sides of the sky fabric by about ¼″.

2. Place the sky fabric horizontally, with the curve side toward the top, on release paper or a pressing sheet. Center the long side of the water fabric just under the long straight side of the sky fabric. Fuse-tack in place.

3. Starting at the top right corner of the long side, cut an extended convex arc across the wheat field fabric to the bottom left corner. Abut the wheat field against the lower right side of the sky fabric, overlapping the water fabric. Fuse-tack in place.

4. Free-cut small looping arcs into both short sides and one long side of the tree line fabric. Vary the height and depth of the loops to create an irregular tree line silhouette. Free-cut the other long side in shallow wave shapes like the waves on water.

5. Center the tree line fabric on the lower edge of the sky fabric, overlapping the sky fabric and covering the joins between the sky, water, and wheat field fabrics. Fuse-tack in place.

6. Clip the swamp fabric about ½" in on a long side. Separate the fabric at the clipped edge, and rip the fabric lengthwise. Fray the ripped edge by about ¼" on the larger piece of fabric by pulling the threads and unweaving the fabric. A straight pin or T-pin helps to separate the threads from the fabric.

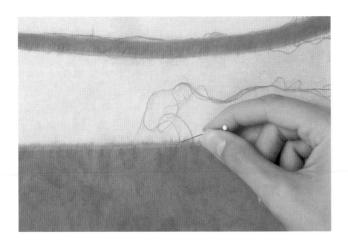

7. Fuse fusible web onto the wrong side of the swamp fabric just up to the frayed edge of the fabric. After the fabric cools, remove the release paper. Use a decorative blade to trim the 2 short sides about ¼". Use a decorative blade to trim the nonfrayed side in a wavy shape.

8. Repeat Step 6 and 7 with the reeds and front field fabrics. Note: It's easy to fray Dupioni silk without ripping it.

9. Place the left corner of the frayed edge of the swamp fabric on the left side of the water where the tree line meets the water. Angle the swamp fabric down to just overlap the bottom edge of the wheat field fabric. Fuse-tack in place.

10. Place the reeds fabric on the swamp fabric at an angle. Repeat with the front field fabric. Fuse-tack in place.

11. Cut the grass fabric square diagonally from corner to corner to form 2 triangles. Cut 3 bias strips measuring about ½" wide from the long bias side of one of the grass triangles. Repeat with the other grass triangle for a total of 6 strips.

12. Cut across each grass bias strip diagonally from corner to corner to form tapered triangular strips that measure ½" wide at one end and that taper to about ¹⁄₃₂" wide for a total of 12 blades of grass.

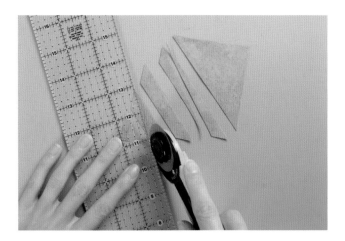

13. Arrange the blades of grass on top of the swamp and fields fabrics. Fuse-tack in place. After the collage cools, remove it from the release paper.

14. Center the landscape collage on the background fabric, and fuse-tack in place.

15. Hold the house fabric horizontally. Snip a triangle from the lower right-hand corner and the upper right-hand corner to form the roof of the house. Place the house on release paper, and fuse-tack in place.

16. Free-cut a blue door, 4 X-shaped orange windows, and 2 skinny gold roof lines from the architectural features fabrics. Decorate the house with the architectural features, and fuse-tack in place. After the fabric cools, remove it from the release paper. Place the house on the background fabric, and fuse-tack in place.

17. Center the quilt top on the batting, and press in place.

COMPLETING THE PROJECT

Refer to pages 54–60 for complete descriptions of quilting and finishing techniques.

1. Use Wrapped Binding #1 (page 57) to quilt and finish the quilt.

2. Add a hanging loop (page 59).

Completing the Creation:
FINISHING TOUCHES FOR FUSED JOURNAL QUILTS

Here are the final steps to complete your beautiful creations. Learn about quilting, binding, and displaying your fast2fuse quilt, and proudly join the alumni of the Chicago School of Fusing!

QUILTING THE FAST2FUSE QUILT

Quilting by Hand

Hand embroidery and quilting enhance the surface of the small journal quilt. They invite the viewer closer and add texture, pattern, and spark to the quilt top. Although hand stitching through fast2fuse is possible, I recommend hand stitching the quilt top through the batting **before** attaching it to fast2fuse (see *Object of My Affection*, page 20). The stitched top and batting are then treated as one piece when you finish and bind the quilt.

Limit fused fabrics to two or three layers when stitching by hand. Simple stitches like a running stitch, cross-stitch, seed stitch, and French knots give the best results. The quilts in this book were stitched with my own hand-dyed size 8 and size 12 Pearl cotton thread from Artfabrik, Inc. (see Resources, page 63).

1. Complete the quilt top, and place it on the *non-scrim* side of the batting.

Tip

Some cotton battings have a scrim, or stabilizing coating, applied to one side. Applying fused fabrics to the scrim side of the batting may shrink the scrim and ripple the surface of the quilt. The ripples cannot be steamed flat. If you're not sure which side is the scrim side, test the batting before use.

2. Steam set (page 11) the quilt top to the batting.

3. Stitch with size 5, 8, or 12 Pearl cotton thread and the appropriate-size hand embroidery needle. I generally use sizes 1–5.

4. Refer to Binding the fast2fuse Quilt (page 57) for binding options.

ILLINOIS TREES #8, 13" × 13", Laura Wasilowski
Hand quilt through the batting and quilt top, not through the fast2fuse.

PRINCESS LOUISE POPPIES #2, 13″ × 13″, Laura Wasilowski
A sewing machine easily stitches through fast2fuse.

Quilting by Machine

Note: With these small fast2fuse quilts, the binding may be done before the quilting.

Fused journal quilts are usually made up of organic shapes, not the geometric shapes found in pieced quilts. Reaching these odd nooks and crannies requires a different type of quilting: free-motion machine stitching. In free-motion stitching, the feed dogs of the sewing machine are dropped, a free-motion foot is placed on the machine, and the stitching is advanced by moving the quilt beneath the needle with your hands. It is like drawing by moving a piece of paper under a stationary pencil.

Learning to free-motion quilt from a qualified instructor is well worth the time. The technique takes practice, but the results are stunning. Free-motion work is not only functional,

but it also adds another dimension to your art, another layer of interest for the viewer. But before you even thread your sewing machine for free-motion work, you must plan the stitching for your quilt.

THINK BEFORE YOU STITCH

Plan a free-motion stitch route that lets you sew continuously without changing thread color or stopping the needle. Use your finger to trace the stitch path on the surface of the quilt. Look for the shortest transition between shapes so the connecting stitches between those shapes are not conspicuous. Plan the type of stitches needed such as outline stitches, echo stitches, sketching stitches, patterning stitches, and enclosed stitches (see page 56). And don't forget an escape route, a place to end the stitching.

Tip

One way to plan your quilting is to place a piece of clear vinyl (such as Quilter's Vinyl) on top of your quilt and draw potential quilting designs on the vinyl. You can either keep a design or erase it and try again.

OUTLINE STITCHES

Outlining fused elements with stitching makes the shapes pop out like a bas-relief, or low-relief, sculpture. To make a shape come forward, smoothly guide the needle around the shape, coming as close as you can without stitching on the element. For a subtle outline, select a thread color that blends well with the background colors. For a more emphatic outline, use a thread darker than the background color.

ECHO STITCHES

Echoing the contour of a fabric shape with a decorative edge reinforces that decorative edge and introduces a repetitive motif that causes the illusion of movement on the quilt surface. The embellished fabric edges made with decorative rotary cutter blades are readymade for echo stitching. Follow the shape, stitching on the surface of the shape or next to the shape, echoing the shape's line.

Outline and echo stitches

SKETCHING STITCHES

Free-motion sketching is like drawing on the quilt surface with a pencil. You can add veins to leaves, petals to flowers, and waves to water. For boldly sketched lines, use thread colors that contrast in hue or value with the fused shape.

Sketching stitches

PATTERNING STITCHES

For building texture and filling in open expanses of fabric, patterning stitches are best. You will discover many free-motion quilting designs, but my favorite and the easiest is the MEMEME design. For this design, simply make three vertical peaks of stitching (M) and then three horizontal peaks of stitching (E). MEMEME patterning fits nicely around fused shapes, fills in large areas, and can be varied with additional tilts, knobs, and waves.

MEMEME patterning stitches

ENCLOSED STITCHES

To make enclosed stitches, first outline a large space with stitching. The outline may be in a specific shape, like a leaf or a shape that accommodates a fused shape on the quilt surface. After the space is defined, fill in the interior with patterning or sketching stitches. If you want to add more quilting outside the space, plan an escape route before completely enclosing the space.

Enclosed stitches

BINDING THE FAST2FUSE QUILT

There are three ways to neatly finish the edges of your fast2fuse quilt. For a trimmed binding, simply cut the completed quilt edges with a decorative rotary cutter blade. The two wrapped binding options use fabric that extends from the quilt top or quilt back and wraps around the quilt edges.

Trimmed Binding

Note: This finishing technique is completed before quilting.

1. Layer the backing fabric, fast2fuse, and quilt top. Steam set (page 11) the quilt top and quilt back to the fast2fuse.

2. To even up the edges, trim the quilt with a straight rotary cutter blade, quilting ruler, and cutting mat.

3. Trim the quilt again by about ¼" with a decorative rotary cutter blade.

Trim quilt with decorative blade.

4. Quilt by machine.

Wrapped Binding #1

Note: This finishing technique may be completed before or after quilting.

1. Place the quilt top, right side down, on the ironing surface.

2. Center the fast2fuse on the wrong side of the quilt. If necessary, trim the fast2fuse so it is ¾"–1" smaller than the quilt top on all sides.

Center fast2fuse.

3. Turn the quilt and fast2fuse over, keeping everything in place. Place the fast2fuse on release paper or a pressing sheet. Steam set (page 11) the quilt top. After the fabric cools, remove it from the pressing sheet or release paper.

4. Place the quilt top, right side down, on the ironing surface. Fold a corner of the quilt top fabric at a 45° angle onto the fast2fuse. Leave a little ease at the tip of the corner to get a sharp point. Fuse-tack (page 11) the fabric just at the corner (a small wand iron is handy for this task). Do not get the fast2fuse glue on the iron.

Fold corner, and fuse-tack onto fast2fuse.

5. Repeat Step 4 at each corner of the quilt.

6. At one corner, run your fingernail along each side of the tip of the corner to make a sharp crease in the fabric. Fold one side of the quilt top fabric onto the fast2fuse. Slowly pull, wrap, and fuse-tack the quilt top to the back, following the edge of the fast2fuse. Stop about midway along the edge.

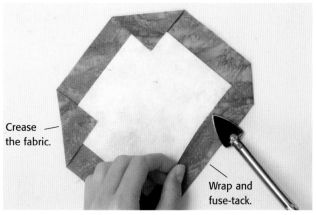

Crease the fabric.

Wrap and fuse-tack.

Wrap and fuse-tack fabric to fast2fuse.

7. At that same corner, fold the adjacent side of the quilt top fabric onto the fast2fuse, making a sharp point at the corner. Slowly pull, wrap, and fuse-tack the quilt top to the back, following the edge of the fast2fuse. Stop about midway along the edge.

Make sharp corner point.

8. Repeat Steps 6–7 around the entire perimeter of the quilt.

9. If you don't want your quilting to show on the back of the quilt, machine quilt now. Otherwise you can quilt after Step 15.

10. Place the quilt top, right side up, on the wrong side of the backing fabric. Make sure the backing fabric is the same size as the quilt top. Trim the backing if necessary. Remove the quilt top.

11. Cut 4 strips of fusible web each measuring about 1″ wide. Cut 2 strips the width of the backing fabric and 2 strips the length of the backing fabric less 2″.

12. Place the strips of fusible web, glue sides down, around the perimeter of the wrong side of the backing fabric. Iron the fusible web in place. After the fabric cools, remove the release paper.

Add fusible web to perimeter of backing.

13. Use a decorative blade to trim about ¼″ from the perimeter of the backing fabric.

14. Center the backing fabric, glue side down, on the back of the quilt. Fuse-tack in place.

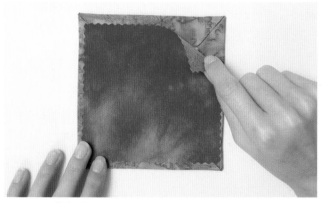

Fuse on quilt back.

15. Steam set the back of the quilt.

16. If you didn't do the quilting in Step 9, do it now.

Wrapped Binding #2

*Note: This finishing technique is completed **before** quilting.*

1. Center the backing fabric, right side up, on top of the fast2fuse. The backing fabric must extend 1″–1½″ beyond the fast2fuse on all sides. Fuse-tack the backing in place.

2. Turn the quilt back and fast2fuse over, keeping everything in place.

3. Repeat Steps 4–8 from Wrapped Binding #1 (pages 57–58) to wrap the edges of the backing fabric to the front of the fast2fuse.

4. Place the quilt top on the fast2fuse, and trim to the same size if necessary. Remove the quilt top.

5. Use a decorative blade to trim the edges of the quilt top ¼"–½".

6. Center the quilt top on the fast2fuse. Fuse-tack in place.

Fuse quilt top onto fast2fuse.

7. Steam set the front and back of the quilt.

8. Quilt by machine.

DISPLAY OPTIONS

The fast2fuse quilt is so lightweight that the traditional rod pocket is not needed. Instead, stitch a simple hanging loop or set of loops to the quilt back. Slip the loop over a picture hangar, and your artwork is on display!

Simple Hanging Loop

1. Locate a point 1½" down from the center of the top edge of the quilt back. Mark the point with a straight pin.

2. Mark 2 points ½" to the left and ½" to the right of the center point with a pencil or marker. Remove the pin.

3. Thread a needle with a heavy thread (such as a size 5 or 8 embroidery thread), and knot one end.

4. Take one stitch into the quilt back at the left point. Extend the thread across to the right point, and take another stitch.

5. Stitch back into the fabric at the right point, and form a knot. Clip the thread.

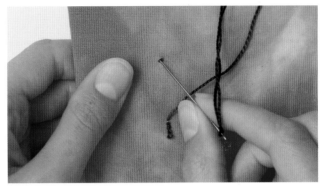

Stitch from point to point, and knot thread.

Alternate Hanging Loops

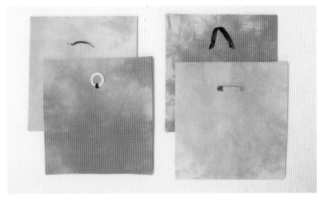

Alternate hanging loops: Chain-stitched loop, plastic loop, ribbon, safety pin

FINAL STEP: Attach a badge from the Chicago School of Fusing to the quilt back.

For more binding techniques, please see my book *Fusing Fun: Fast Fearless Art Quilts*

Patterns

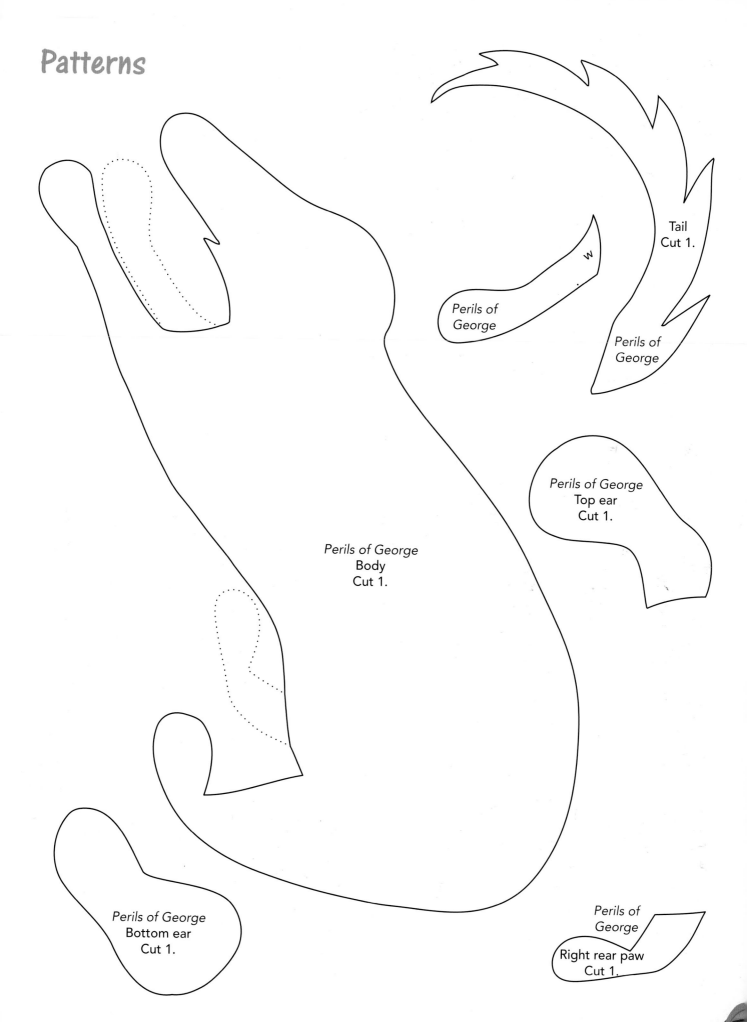

Tail
Cut 1.

Perils of George

Perils of George

Perils of George
Top ear
Cut 1.

Perils of George
Body
Cut 1.

Perils of George
Bottom ear
Cut 1.

Perils of George

Right rear paw
Cut 1.

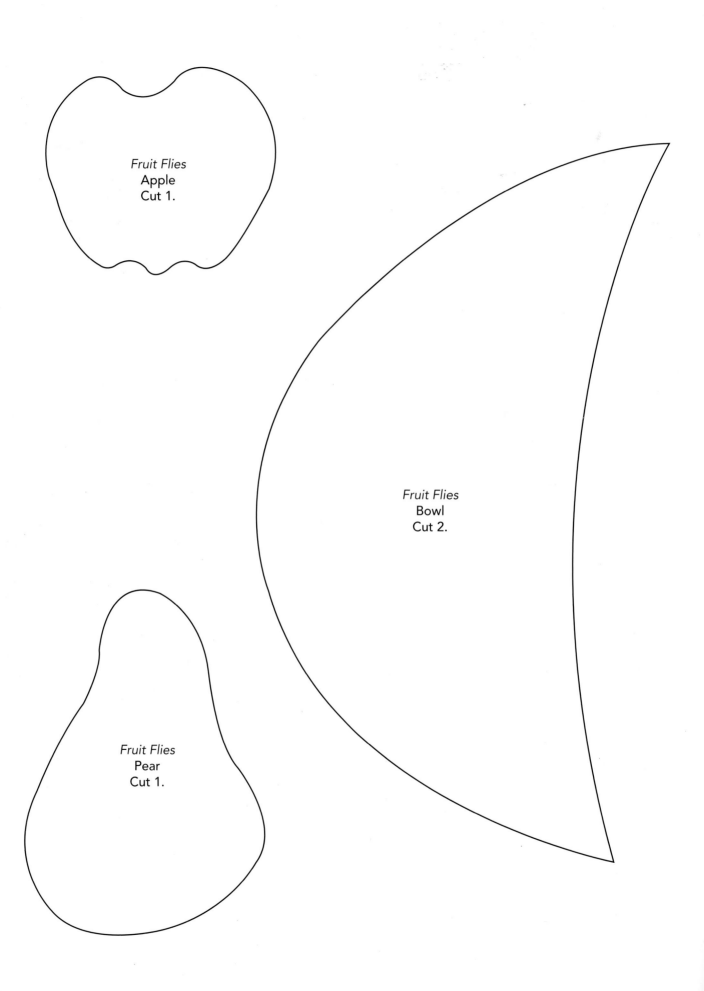

Fruit Flies
Apple
Cut 1.

Fruit Flies
Bowl
Cut 2.

Fruit Flies
Pear
Cut 1.

ABOUT THE AUTHOR

Laura Wasilowski creates art quilts. She is inspired by stories of family, friends, and home. Colorful hand-dyed fabrics and familiar stories combine to make whimsical wall pieces that often chronicle her life.

Laura's artwork is exhibited internationally and displayed in corporate and private collections around the world. She is the owner of the dye shop Artfabrik, and she is a lecturer, a surface designer, a quilt instructor, and the author of *Fusing Fun: Fast Fearless Art Quilts.*

Laura and husband, Steve, live in Elgin, Illinois, and are the proud parents of Gus and Louise.

Also by Laura Wasilowski

RESOURCES

Recommended Reading

Montano, Judith Baker. *Elegant Stitches*. Lafayette, CA: C&T Publishing, 1995.

Wasilowski, Laura. *Fusing Fun: Fast Fearless Art Quilts.* Lafayette, CA: C&T Publishing, 2005.

Appliqué Pressing Sheets

Check your local quilt shop or
BEAR THREAD DESIGNS
P.O. Box 1452
Highland, TX 77562
(281) 462-1799
Email: BearTD@Hotmail.com
Website: www.bearthreaddesigns.com

For More Information

ARTFABRIK, INC. (hand-dyed fabrics and threads)
324 Vincent Place
Elgin, IL 60123
(874) 931-7684
Email: laura@artfabrik.com
Website: www.artfabrik.com

For a list of other fine books from C&T Publishing, and for fast2fuse and Quilter's Vinyl, ask for a free catalog:

C&T PUBLISHING, INC.
P.O. Box 1456
Lafayette, CA 94549
(800) 284-1114
Email: ctinfo@ctpub.com
Website: www.ctpub.com

C&T Publishing's professional photography services are now available to the public. Visit us at www.ctmediaservices.com.

For quilting supplies:

COTTON PATCH
1025 Brown Avenue
Lafayette, CA 94549
(800) 835-4418
(925) 283-7883
Email: CottonPa@aol.com
Website: www.quiltusa.com
Note: Fabrics used in the quilts shown may not be currently available, as fabric manufacturers keep most fabrics in print for only a short time.

Great Titles from C&T PUBLISHING

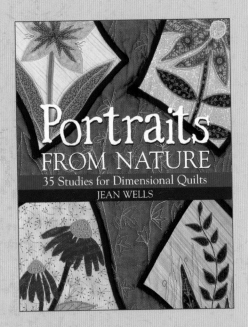

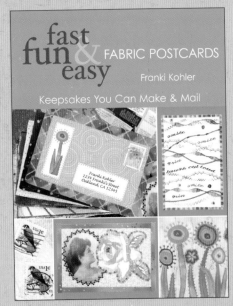